WINDOWS TO A
Mother's Heart

A Special Gift

to:

_____

from:

_____

date:

_____

Copyright © 2003
Brownlow
6309 Airport Freeway
Fort Worth, TX 76117

ISBN: 1-59177-009-2

Printed in Singapore

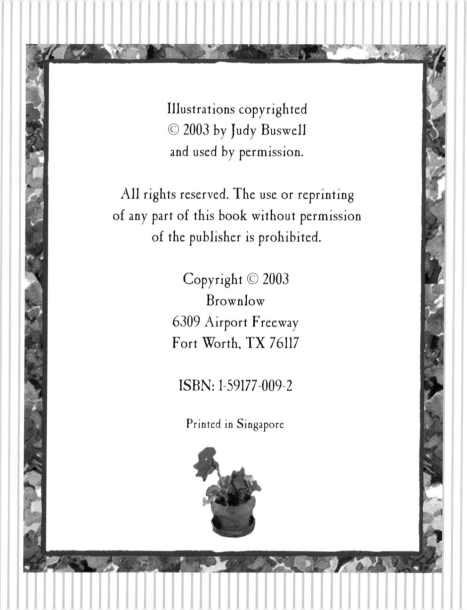

WINDOWS TO A
Mother's Heart

ILLUSTRATED BY *Judy Buswell*

WRITTEN & EDITED BY *Caroline Brownlow*

Brownlow

Children have neither past nor future; they enjoy the present, which very few of us do. LaBRUYERE

Just One Touch

Everybody knows that a good mother gives her children a feeling of trust and stability. She is their earth. She is the one they can count on for the things that matter most of all. She is their food and their bed and the extra blanket when it grows cold in the night; she is their warmth and their health and their shelter; she is the one they want to be near when they cry.

She is the only person in the whole world or in a whole lifetime who can be these things to her children. There is no substitute for her. Somehow even her clothes feel different to her children's hands from anybody else's clothes. Only to touch her skirt or her sleeve makes a troubled child feel better.

KATHERINE BUTLER HATHAWAY

A Mother's Prayer

Lord, give me patience when wee hands

Tug at me with their small demands.

Give me gentle and smiling eyes;

Keep my lips from hasty replies.

Let not weariness, confusion, or noise

Obscure my vision of life's fleeting joys.

So, when in years to come, my house is still—

No bitter memories its rooms may fill.

Of all the rights of women, the greatest is to be a mother.

LIN YUTANG

The earth is the Lord's and everything in it.

PSALM 24:1

Those who dwell among the beauties and

mysteries of the earth are never alone or weary of life.

AUTHOR UNKNOWN

$\mathcal{A}$ young boy was served canned corn for dinner. Looking up
hopefully, he advised his mother, "I really would like it
better on a 'roller'."

$\mathcal{S}$urely, we all need a closed place
wherein we may strike root and,
like the seed, *become*.

ANTOINE DE SAINT-EXUPERY

$\mathcal{C}$hildren do not know how their parents
love them, and they never will 'til they
have children of their own.

COOKE

$\mathcal{T}$hese are the children God has given me.
God has been good to me....

GENESIS 33:5

On Earth There Is No Other

There is but one and only one,

Whose love will fail you never.

One who lives from sun to sun,

With constant fond endeavor.

There is but one and only one,

On earth there is no other.

In heaven a noble work was done,

When God gave us a Mother.

God

I Took His Hand

My dishes went unwashed today, I didn't make the bed,
I took his hand and followed where his eager footsteps led.

Oh, yes, we went adventuring, my little son and I...
Exploring all the great outdoors beneath the summer sky.

We waded in a crystal stream, we wandered through a wood...
My kitchen wasn't swept today, but life was rich and good.

We found a cool, sun-dappled glade, and now my small son knows
How mother bunny hides her nest, where jack-in-the-pulpit grows.

We watched a robin feed her young, we climbed a sunlit hill...
Saw cloud-sheep scamper through the sky, we plucked a daffodil.

That my house was neglected, that I didn't brush the stairs,
In twenty years no one on earth will know or even care.

But that I've helped my little boy to noble manhood grow
In twenty years the whole wide world may look and see and know.

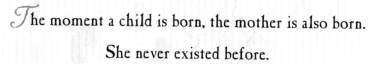

The moment a child is born, the mother is also born.

She never existed before.

The woman existed, but the mother, never.

A mother is something absolutely new.

RAJNEESH

Motherhood is priced of God, at price no man

may dare to lesson or misunderstand.

HELEN HUNT JACKSON

We carry with us the wonders we seek without us.

SIR THOMAS BROWNE

Our happiness is greatest

when we cultivate

the happiness of others.

Just when a mother thinks her work is done, she becomes a grandmother. ANONYMOUS

*F*or the mother is and must be, whether she knows it or not,

the greatest, strongest and most lasting teacher her children have.

HANNAH WHITALL SMITH

*Y*ou know children are growing up

when they start asking questions that have answers.

JOHN J. PLOMP

*T*hose who sow seeds of kindness will have a perpetual harvest.

ANONYMOUS

*G*od sends children to enlarge our hearts; and to make us

unselfish and full of kindly sympathies and affections.

M. HOWITT

Flowers for Mom

Last spring, my two grandsons,
Blaze and Beaux, wanted to pick wildflowers
in the park to give their Mom.

There was no special occasion — and they were just wilted wildflowers clenched in two chubby fists — but to Mom they were priceless! Moms are like that. They accept our humble, simple tributes as if they were gold enough for a king. And in so doing, moms teach us to be more loving, more giving, and more full of gratitude.

CAROLINE BROWNLOW

Our children are likely to live up to what we believe of them.

LADY BIRD JOHNSON

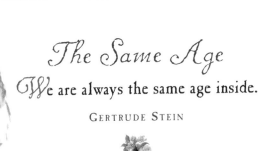

The Same Age

We are always the same age inside.

GERTRUDE STEIN

Some lives, like evening primroses,

blossom most beautifully in the evening of life.

C.E. COWEN

Those who love deeply never grow old.

SIR ARTHUR WING PINERO

We are young at any age, if we are planning for tomorrow. ANONYMOUS

The mother love is like God's love;

He loves us not because we are lovable,

but because it is His nature to love,

and because we are His children.

EARL RINEY

God's love

Use the talents you have;
for the woods would be silent
if no birds sang except the best.

As she left the hospital, a new mother asked the nurse,

"What will be the most difficult thing for me to learn?"

The wise nurse replied, "That other people have perfect children too".

ANONYMOUS

There is an amazed curiosity in every young mother.

It is strangely miraculous to see and to hold a living being formed

within oneself and issued forth from oneself.

SIMONE DE BEAUVOIR

A new mother once asked a pediatrician what was

the best time to put her children to bed.

He replied, "While you still have the strength."

ANONYMOUS

There's Only One

Most of all the beautiful things
in life come by twos and threes, by
dozens and hundreds. Plenty of roses,
stars, sunsets, rainbows, brothers and
sisters, aunts and cousins, but only
one mother in the whole world.

KATE DOUGLAS WIGGINS

Mother's love grows by giving. CHARLES LAMB

Always Use Lots of Sugar

As a newlywed, I thought I knew how to cook everything. After all, my grandmother, Mamaw Darwin, had taught me "the secret recipe." As she often said, "Carol, if you want to make things taste really good, always use lots of sugar."

The first autumn after our honeymoon, I decided to cook apples. As they simmered in the pan, I was ready for the crowning touch of my success — I poured two heaping scoops of sugar on the two tiny apples and finished cooking them.

In a few minutes, I proudly spooned the apples into a serving dish. They looked so delicious — but we never got to eat them. As soon as I put a spoon in them they candied and crystalized into something that looked like brown cement. We had to break the bowl just to get the spoon out.

In spite of the ill-fated apples and the broken bowl, I still like Mamaw's advice — "just add sugar." In fact over the years, I've learned that her secret formula works on nearly everything around the house: children, pets, friends — yes, even husbands.

CAROLINE BROWNLOW

The Mender

A mother is a mender. She mends socks, clothes and broken dolls. She mends furniture, clocks and venetian blinds. Sometimes she fixes broken bike chains and other things that "come loose" in life. But most often she mends a child's broken heart or a daddy's broken spirit. She puts crushed feelings back together again and glues them tight with a drop of super-love. Sometimes she mends a little bird's broken wing or removes a grass burr from a puppy's foot. She is, in her own gentle way, a minister of mending, and she takes her ministry very seriously. She goes about her mending with words of kindness, acts of love and the healing balm of compassion. She's a mender because she's a mother.

MARY HOLLINGSWORTH

She watches over the affairs of her household. PROVERBS 31:27

The best thing mothers can spend on their children is time, not money.

"Mama, Watch Me"

Every person needs recognition and approval. At first the toddler says, "Mama, watch me." as he or she jumps off the porch step or turns a flip in the grass. Through the years, mother "watches" and nods approval and joy as we grow and mature. And while we may become too sophisticated to ask for it, we still seek approval and recognition. We all do — no matter how old we are.

CAROLINE BROWNLOW

*F*lowers always make people better, happier, and more useful;

they are sunshine, food and medicine to the soul.

LUTHER BURBANK

*A*s a mother comforts her child, so I will comfort you.

ISAIAH 66:13

*A*void pressing problems. Wash and dry children's clothes

and leave them in the ironing basket until the kids outgrow them.

PEGGY GOLDTRAP

What Is a Mother?

Somewhere between the youthful energy of a teenager and the golden years of a woman's life, there lives a marvelous and loving person known as "Mother."

A mother is a curious mixture of patience, kindness, understanding, discipline, industriousness, purity, and love. A mother can be, at one and the same time, both "lovelorn counselor" to a heartsick daughter and "head football coach" to an athletic son.

A mother can sew the tiniest stitch in the material for that dainty prom dress, and she is equally experienced in threading through the heaviest traffic with a station wagon.

A mother is the only creature on earth who can cry when she's happy, laugh when she's heartbroken, and work when she's feeling ill.

A mother is as gentle as a lamb and as strong as a giant. Only a mother can appear so weak and helpless and yet be the same one who puts the fruit jar cover on so tightly even Dad can't get it off.

A mother is a picture of helplessness when Dad is near and a marvel of resourcefulness when she's all alone.

A mother has the angelic voice of a member in the celestial choir as she sings Brahms' lullaby to a babe held tight in her arms, yet this same voice can dwarf the sound of an amplifier when she calls her boys in for supper.

A mother has the fascinating ability to be almost everywhere at once, and she alone can somehow squeeze an enormous amount of living into an average day.

A mother is "old-fashioned" to her teenager, just "Mom" to her third-grader, and simply "Mama" to little two-year-old sister.

But there is no greater thrill in life than to point to that wonderful woman and be able to say to all the world, "That's my mother!"

FRED KRUSE

Children and flowers
both blossom
when showered with love.

Motherhood is being available to your children whenever they need you, no matter what their age or their need.

DORIS PENGILLY

$\mathcal{L}$ove is a seed: it has only to sprout, and its roots spread far and wide.

ANTOINE DE SAINT-EXUPERY

$\mathcal{T}$he woman who creates and sustains a home

and under whose hands children grow up to be strong and pure men

and women, is a creator second only to God.

HELEN HUNT JACKSON

$\mathcal{C}$hildren despise their parents until the age of forty, when they

suddenly become just like them, thus preserving the system.

QUENTIN CREWE

$\mathcal{H}$er children arise and call her blessed.

PROVERBS 31:28

A mother holds

her children's hands

for a while,

their hearts forever.

ANONYMOUS

Clothed with Kindness

It is possible to have compassion without love,
and it is possible to have kindness without love; but it is
impossible for one who has put on love to be unkind and
without compassion, for love itself is not just an accessory
garment. Love is the complete garment that has all the
others built into it, so that love is a total way of life.

RAY ANDERSON

Clothe yourselves with compassion, kindness, humility, gentleness and patience.
Over all these virtues, put on love, which binds them all together in perfect unity.
COLOSSIANS 3:12, 14

May the Lord make you increase,

both you and your children. May you be blessed

by the Lord, the maker of heaven and earth.

PSALM 115: 14, 15

Let There Be Mama

Let there be sunshine.

Let there be blue skies.

Let there be Mama.

Let there be me.

OLD RUSSIAN FOLK SONG

*P*eople who say they sleep like a baby usually don't have one.

LEO J. BURKE

A person who respects the Lord will have security.

And his children will be protected.

PROVERBS 14:26

*H*ome is where one starts from.

T.S. ELIOT

Once Upon a Memory

Once upon a memory,

Someone wiped away a tear,

Held me close and loved me.

Thank you, Mother dear.

ANONYMOUS

No man is poor who has had a godly mother.

ABRAHAM LINCOLN

Like a Garden

Her heart is like her garden,

Old-fashioned, quaint and sweet,

With here a wealth of blossoms,

And there a still retreat.

ALICE E. ALLEN

A mother understands what a child does not say.

OLD PROVERB

*M*any make the household but only one the home.

JAMES RUSSELL LOWELL

*N*ever let the good things of life rob you of the best things.

M.D. BABCOCK

*M*other is the name for God in the lips and hearts of little children.

WILLIAM MAKEPEACE THACKERAY

*W*hen a mother forgives, she kisses the offense

into everlasting forgetfulness.

HENRY WARD BEECHER

Mother's Love

Her love is like an island
In life's ocean, vast and wide,
A peaceful, quiet shelter
From the wind, and rain, and tide.

'Tis bound on the north by Hope,
By Patience on the west,
By tender Counsel on the south,
And on the east by Rest.

Above it like a beacon light
Shine faith, and truth, and prayer;
And through the changing
scenes of life,
I find a haven there.

AUTHOR UNKNOWN

The beautiful is as usefu

the useful, perhaps more so.

Victor Hugo

To my mother I tell the truth. I have no thought,

no feeling that I cannot share with my mother,

and she is like a second conscience to me, her eyes

like a mirror reflecting my own image.

WILLIAM GERHARDI

Cheerfulness is the atmosphere in which all things thrive.

JEAN PAUL RICHTER

God invented a mother's heart,
and He certainly has the pattern in His own.

HARRIET BEECHER STOWE

There's nothing wrong with teenagers
that reasoning with them won't aggravate.

When

the children are

grown and gone,

A mother's

love goes

on and on.

I Love You, Mom

I love you not only for what you are, but for what I am when I am with you. I love you not only for what you have made of yourself, but for what you are making of me. I love you for the part of me that you bring out.

I love you for putting your hand into my heaped-up heart, and passing over all the foolish and frivolous and weak things which you cannot help dimly seeing there, and for drawing out into the light all the beautiful, radiant belongings, that no one else had looked quite far enough to find.

I love you for ignoring the possibilities of the fool and weakling in me, and for laying firm hold on the possibilities of good in me. I love you for closing your eyes to the discords in me, and for adding to the music in me by worshipful listening.

I love you because you have done more than any creed could have done to make me good, and more than any fate could have done to make me happy. You have done it just by being yourself. Perhaps that is what being a mom means after all.

ANONYMOUS

All the flowers of
all the tomorrows are in
the seeds of today.

ANONYMOUS

$\mathcal{W}$e spend the first three years of a child's life teaching him to walk and talk and the next fifteen teaching him to sit down and be quiet!

ANONYMOUS

$\mathcal{O}$pen my eyes Lord that I may see wonderful things.

PSALM 119:18

$\mathcal{T}$here is in all this world no fount of deep, strong, deathless love, save that within a mother's heart.

FELICIA HEMANS

$\mathcal{I}$t is not the outside riches but the inside ones that produce happiness.

FOLK WISDOM

If you have love in your heart,

you will always have something to give.

It will be gone before you know it.

The fingerprints on the wall appear higher and higher,

then suddenly they disappear.

DOROTHY EVSLIN

The greatest work that you will ever do

will be within the four walls of your home.

ANONYMOUS

A life without love is like a garden without flowers.

ANONYMOUS

Those who give love,

gather love.

Windows of Love

*L*ove does not consist in gazing at each other,

but in looking together in the same direction.

ANTOINE DE SAINT-EXUPERY

*W*e are shaped and fashioned by what we love.

JOHANN VON GOETHE

*L*ove always protects, always trusts, always hopes, always perseveres.

I CORINTHIANS 13:7

*Y*ou can give without loving, but you cannot love without giving.

AMY CARMICHAEL

More Than I Know

Mother, I love you so. Said the child,

I love you more than I know.

She laid her head on her mother's arm

And the love between them kept her warm.

STEVIE SMITH

Dear Mom,

*I*t is said that a mother is supposed

to be the one through whom God

whispers love to His little children.

Just in case I never told you,

yes, Mom, I heard the whispers.